Drawing the Figure
from Top to Toe

Drawing the Figure
FROM TOP TO TOE

by Arthur Zaidenberg

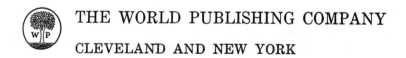
THE WORLD PUBLISHING COMPANY

CLEVELAND AND NEW YORK

Published by The World Publishing Company
2231 West 110th Street, Cleveland, Ohio 44102

Published simultaneously in Canada by
Nelson, Foster & Scott Ltd.

Library of Congress Catalog Card Number: 66-22550

FIRST EDITION

FOR TOMMY

Contents

Foreword

FOR THE STUDENT to have a deep respect for good art and good artists is natural and, were it lacking, that lack would show in the student's work.

However, there is found too often in students a reverence for the mature artist and his developed craftsmanship that intimidates the novice to the point of inhibiting him.

The results are the often-heard laments on the part of the student that go something like this: "I'll never be that good. I'll never draw that well. Who am I to reach such heights?"

The fact is that relatively few art students reach the heights of creativeness of the great masters. On the other hand, thousands of students with faith in their own potential, the will to study and practice, love of the craft, and the honest desire to "say something" in art develop every year and add to our pleasure and understanding of the world around us.

Go to museums and exhibitions. Look at the many splendid art books now available in every library. Study the masters and enjoy the fine work of contemporary artists. Learn from them, love them, and respect them. Then, go home to your studio and be yourself. Vanity and ego in controlled quantities are indispensable ingredients to the artist and must be part of the student's approach to his work.

In the process of technical study acquire what you need from these pages and from other sources of information that will aid you in the development of simplicity, dexterity, and ease in the use of the artist's tools.

But remember this during your studies: Remain true to your own viewpoint and handwriting.

You may not become a great artist or even a very good one. On the other hand, you may.

Whatever happens, you will have a very good time trying, and you will learn to look at things about you with the artist's eye, a valid reason in itself for the study of art.

Materials for Drawing

ARTISTS, BEING CREATIVE, as a consequence are adventurous and inventive. I have known hundreds of artists and have always found them to be tremendously interested in trying new materials and inventing combinations of materials to obtain striking and daring variations in their drawing techniques.

Study the drawings of the old masters and you will find that none of them were content to use the commonplace materials of their time. They experimented with chalks, crayons, sepia inks, leads of various degrees of softness, and innumerable other drawing materials and combinations of them.

The drawings in this book were made with ordinary lead pencils, Conte crayons, India inks applied with brush or pen, carbon pencils, and combinations of several of these in some drawings.

Be experimental in your use of materials. You may find that your lines are stilted and restricted in one medium and free in another. Find the ones most comfortable for your purposes and then do not restrict yourself only to those but go on experimenting with others. You will get much pleasure from trying new media and will find fresh sources of expression.

Introduction

THE HUMAN FIGURE has been of absorbing interest through the ages to all people in all areas of the world.

It has been extolled by poets, sung by troubadours, pampered by athletes, covered and spurned by moralists, praised by architects and engineers, adored by lovers, and has been the consuming subject of study by medical scientists. For painters and sculptors it was the main source of inspiration for five thousand years, interrupted only by the recent twenty- to thirty-year period when nonobjective painting and sculpture made the human figure taboo as a subject worthy of the preoccupation of artists. The unlamented demise—to many—of this art period has again brought the human figure into repute and artists are once more involving themselves in the study and portrayal of the nude and clothed body.

Some choose to depict the body in terms of realism, others use it as a point of reference for their flights of fancy into abstract concepts and emotional expressions that often result in statements "larger than life." Such creative departures are the right and indeed the function of the artist. The statements made have richly diversified our art heritage and will certainly enrich our future art experiences.

That the human figure should be material for the artist which is more conducive to emotional expression than other objects in nature is not surprising. The body's joys, its pains, its youth and aging, its physical pleasures and ecstasy are certainly vital subjects for art expressions.

The seminude body is also coming into good repute as sensible bathing suits allowing for freedom of movement and healthful exposure to the sun and air replace the Mother Hubbards of the not too remote past. Women's clothes are more adapted to the human form instead of retaining a tentlike quality intended to hide the body rather than join in its life activities.

The noble Greek art of the Golden Age gave to the nude the dignity it deserves without any suggestion of pin-up lasciviousness, and the modern artist's approach must be in the same vein.

As drawing from the nude returns to vogue, the contemporary artist must learn or relearn the body's construction and its character.

Here in these pages the elements of figure drawing will be reviewed and a number of approaches to drawing styles will be examined. These suggested approaches are by no means to be considered *the* way to draw. Each student inevitably has his own handwriting and this must not be suppressed in order to attempt to emulate the "styles" of drawing shown here. Far more important than the successful copying of anyone else's style of drawing or technique is the personal statement of each student.

The simplifications, the analysis of pose and structure, the basic approaches demonstrated here may be studied and absorbed with profit to the student. Beyond that point the artist within should take over and personal expression should be given free rein.

Simplification

THROUGHOUT THIS BOOK the words "simplify," "eliminate," and "generalize" will appear frequently. The reasons for these repeated admonitions must be made clear at the outset.

The forms of nature are infinitely complex and vastly prolific.

The student and the artist have only a short life and have much to accomplish during that life. *Ars longa, vita brevis,* the often-quoted saying, while it really means, "Art is lasting, life is brief" may be paraphrased to mean, "Art requires much time and the artist doesn't have enough to waste!" But the brevity of our lives and the vastness of art studies are not the main reasons for the three commandments above.

The fact is that good drawing is the opposite of faithful copying of the infinite details of nature. The artist accentuates and omits. He chooses and discards. He seeks the pertinent, not the obvious. *He* must be judge and jury of that which he sees, and it is his comment upon it rather than his reproduction of it that makes a good drawing.

This is not to imply that the recognizable representation of nature is undesirable, a point reached by many contemporary artists. It means that the artist's function is to create and that process must be foremost in his mind. Slavish copying of nature's details will not serve that end.

Gertrude Stein said of Picasso, "The difference between Picasso and inferior painters is that inferior painters put in all the leaves on a tree, with the result that you can see neither tree nor leaves. Picasso paints one leaf on a tree, and you see the life of the tree."

And, to quote Edith Sitwell, "The child and the great artist—these alone receive the sensation fresh as it was at the beginning of the world."

One more pertinent quote—Roger Fry, writing of the postimpressionists, says, "These artists do not seek to imitate life, but to find an equivalent for life. . . ."

THE EYE IS AN ARTIST

The theory that "anyone can draw" is one I have long held to be true and one that is supported by many manifestations. Earlier in this book I pointed out the undeniable fact that almost everyone is able to learn to write flowing script, which requires a high degree of dexterity and co-ordination. Many people write a beautiful script, uniquely their own, that indicates fine creative individuality. Whether beautiful or not, the handwriting of each of us is unique.

I wish to add another indication of the pictorial creativeness inherent in everyone. That is the curious and delightful creativity of the eye. The eye does not merely see. It tranfers into pictorial terms that which actually does not exist in nature. Objects seen at a distance are not really smaller than those close to the eye. Roads do not really converge nor do objects become darker or lighter because they are near. These are creative optical inventions. They are the pictorial story, not merely the reflection of physical facts.

In nature, edges of all three-dimensional objects are never actually erased by light or shade, but on the retina of the eye the interplay of light tells a story quite different from the immutable, indestructible character of matter. Light and shadow exist, but their beauty and playful dance is registered only in the eye of the beholder.

Given this creative vision and the manual dexterity described at the outset, how can there be any doubt of the artistic potential inherent in us all? Add to this potential the need to say something in art terms, an atmosphere conducive to the saying, and audiences receptive to art, and the world will have more and perhaps greater art than ever before. There cannot be too much art and there can easily be greater art periods.

ANATOMY

The study of human anatomy for art purposes has always been controversial. How much inner structure does an artist need to study in order to draw vital human figures?

In a recent movie based on Irving Stone's historical novel, *The Agony and the Ecstasy,* Michelangelo, through the medium of Mr. Stone's pen and improbable guess, says, when the opportunity of dissection of dead bodies is denied him, "How can I establish a figure, even the crudest outline, if I don't know what I'm doing? How can I achieve anything but surface skin sculpture, exterior curves, outlines of bones, a few muscles brought into play? Effects. What do I know of causes?" We do know that Michelangelo did some clandestine dissection of cadavers, but it is extremely doubtful that such a lament was ever lamented.

The ancient Greeks managed to sculpt magnificent figures without the use of dissection laboratories. Thousands of other splendid artists treating the human figure before and after Michelangelo produced very fine figure paintings and sculpture without such clinical experience.

In fact, during the period of the stringent Victorian art academies, the study of interior anatomy was available through overly detailed charts compiled by scientific anatomists. The resultant effect upon the figures drawn by these art students was stultifying. Too much knowledge had become a dangerous thing.

The drawing of humans requires understanding of their humanity, their passions, their joys, and of the actions they perform that are dictated by mental and emotional sources and not merely by the mechanics of internal anatomy. Michelangelo was especially capable of expressing these human qualities in his work.

It must be understood that this is not a dissertation against the study of human anatomy. A knowledge of the basic bone structure and some muscles can do no harm and can contribute to the drawing of well-proportioned figures whose physical actions are anatomically possible.

For such purpose a short study of skeletal forms and the main close-to-the-surface muscles can be of considerable help. Here we have a few anatomical charts that have been reduced to the bare essentials. In keeping with the theory that the chief elements to be studied in drawing the living figure are the character of the person drawn and intention of the pose assumed, included among the charts of anatomy and basic figures are some comparisons with animal structure and movement.

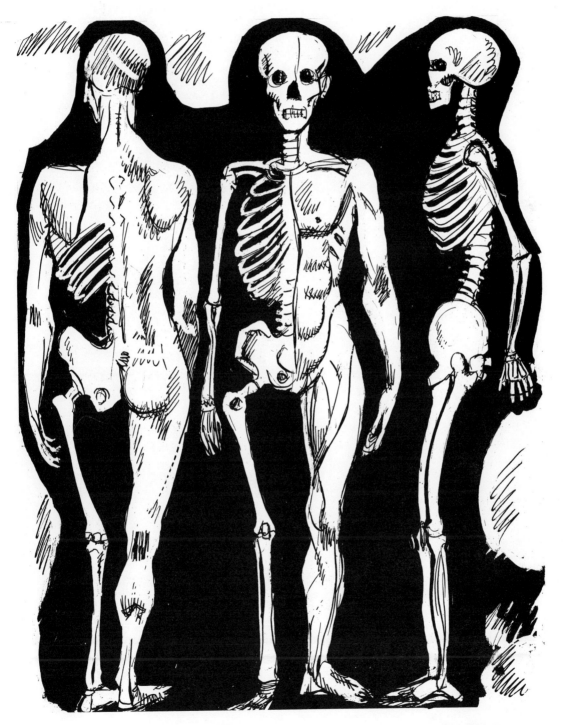

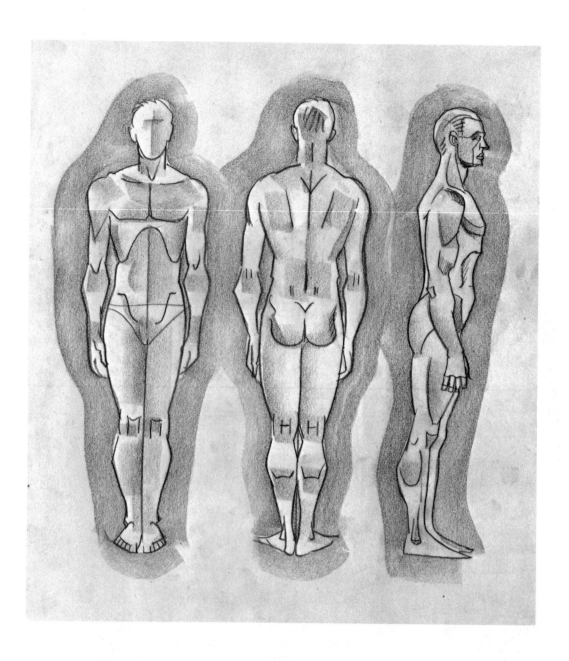

While the opportunities for study of the internal anatomy of wild animals are severely limited, great animal painters have always relied upon close observance of movements and, even more important, the emotional character of the animal. Its stealth and potential ferocity, its alertness and speed, these and many other characteristics tell the animal story far more dramatically and essentially than the static truths of their internal anatomy.

Observe these animals in actions related to those of humans. You will see that although the anatomy of propulsion, the articulation of joints, and muscular movements are similar, the emotional impulses are quite different, and these are the artist's chief concern. The expression of this emotional character most successfully portrays the animal in artistic terms when it is exaggerated.

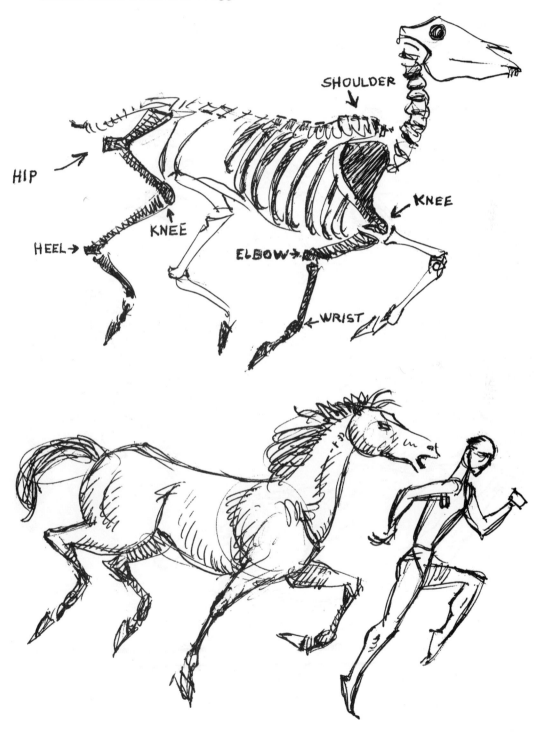

It is the same in drawing humans. It was certainly true in the case of Michelangelo's humans. He exaggerated the action and power of his figures far beyond their anatomic limitations to suit his purpose, and he never hesitated to distort when it served his storytelling of the character.

Use your mental dissecting scalpel to find the essential humanity of the person you are drawing. Add to this the basic proportions and reasonably true anatomic details and you will make drawings of the figure in terms of an artist.

BALANCE

Many anatomists contend that man's true position should be, like that of most animals, on all fours. They attribute many of man's ailments to the so-called false stance of the upright position. Be that as it may, our present natural position for walking, standing, or running is upright, no matter what our prehistoric ancestors did.

The balance of man's body allows for sustained, fluid movement in action even though the actions of walking and running are a series of falls and recoveries. You have only to observe the awkward stagger of a horse or other four-legged animal when attempting to walk on two feet to enable you to compare the balance of man to any other animal.

This balance should be "true" in all your drawing of the figure, no matter what the action is. In examining an action before drawing it, find the "line of balance," the center-of-gravity line that runs through the figure. The line is not visible, but you can learn to trace it by examining a pose to determine where the weight is sustained and what counterbalances are exerted to prevent falling when parts of the body lean away from the perpendicular.

ARTICULATION— MAN AND ANIMAL

The articulation of the limbs of animals and men are similar but man's are considerably more varied in their possible movements. This is not because of a more complex anatomy, but because of the development of man's agility and manual skills through brain-dictated practice.

While we are not capable of running with the speed of an antelope or a cheetah or of springing with the power of a leopard, we can perform highly intricate dance steps, controlled athletic actions, and dexterous movements that, generally speaking, are far beyond the capabilities of animals. The artist, in drawing man's actions, should above all understand the motive and emotion behind each action; for those, the chief controls, anatomy is only the servant, and very often a reluctant one.

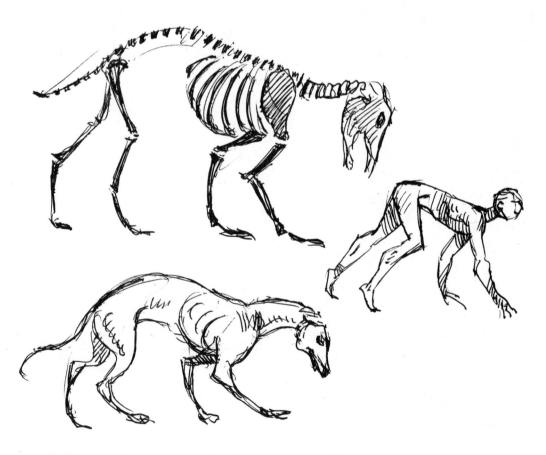

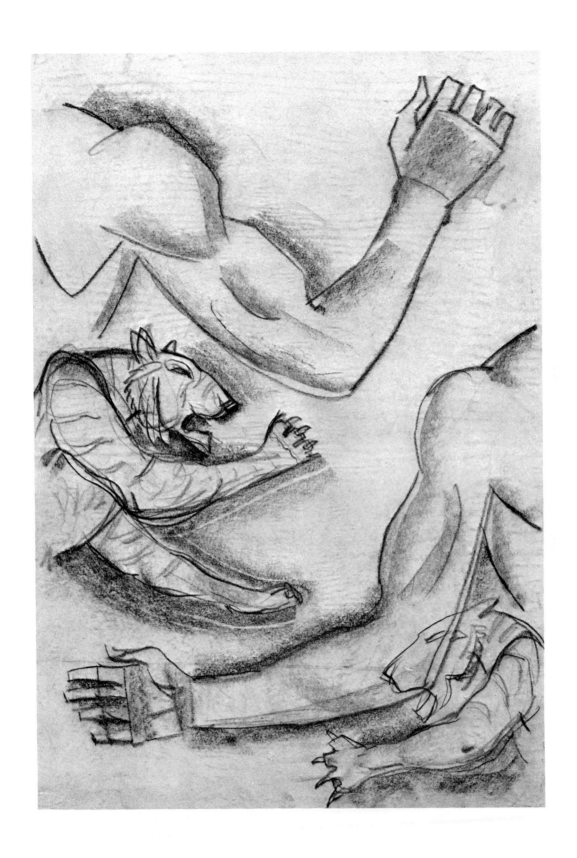

Since Cézanne, many artists have begun to see forms in nature in terms different from the anatomical standpoint. The cubists, especially, have evolved for us a vital viewpoint. This is the concept that artists must see nature in terms of externals rather than from the "inside out" as the academic anatomists did.

The cubists' form was seen geometrically, hence the name for the school of art, cubism.

This viewpoint can be used by the student of the figure. In these pages most of the approaches used in analyzing the pose and structure, as well as the shapes of shadows and the three-dimensional character of the figure, are in terms of geometry.

All things in nature, as well as man-made objects, are, in essence, interpretable in terms of the cube, the cone, the sphere, the tube, and all the variations based on those shapes.

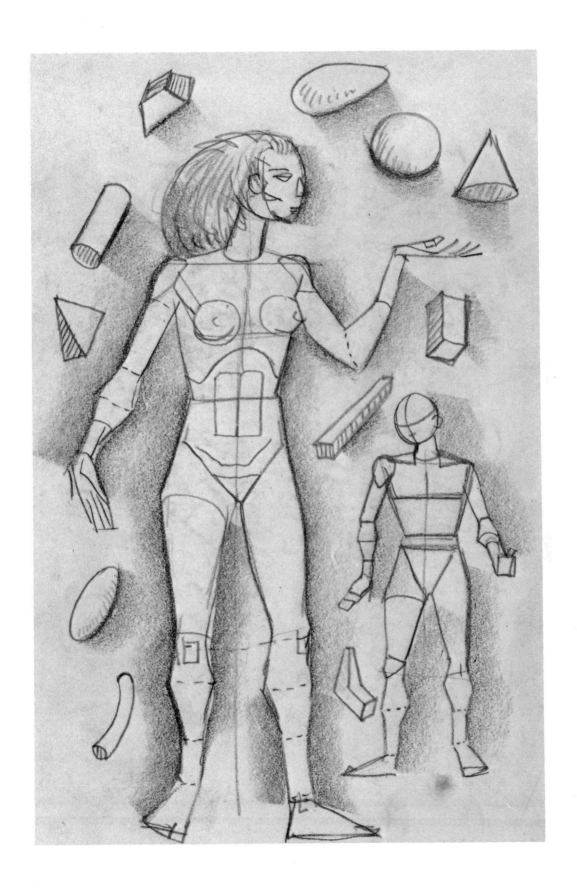

18 **DRAWING THE FIGURE FROM TOP TO TOE**

PERSPECTIVE AND FORESHORTENING

The principles of perspective as applied to drawing are simple, but they call for care in their use. Inexact perspective is painful to the viewer and, unless deliberately used—as is the case among many modern artists—the error can be destructive to an otherwise good drawing or composition.

Since the artist works on a two-dimensional surface, distance, the third dimension, must be implied. The two principles used in implying distance in terms of perspective follow.

1. Upon determining the standpoint of the viewer of a figure or scene, an imaginary horizon is conceived. This imaginary line may either be borne in mind or lightly indicated. It *always* lies at the eye level of the spectator.
   Toward this horizon, things seen recede from the viewer's eye. The boundaries of objects receding into the distance apparently narrow as they move toward the horizon. This process is called converging.
2. As objects recede toward the horizon they appear to diminish in size.

These two basic eye-deceiving methods allow the viewer to "believe" that a penetration of the flat surface has been achieved. Distance has been implied.

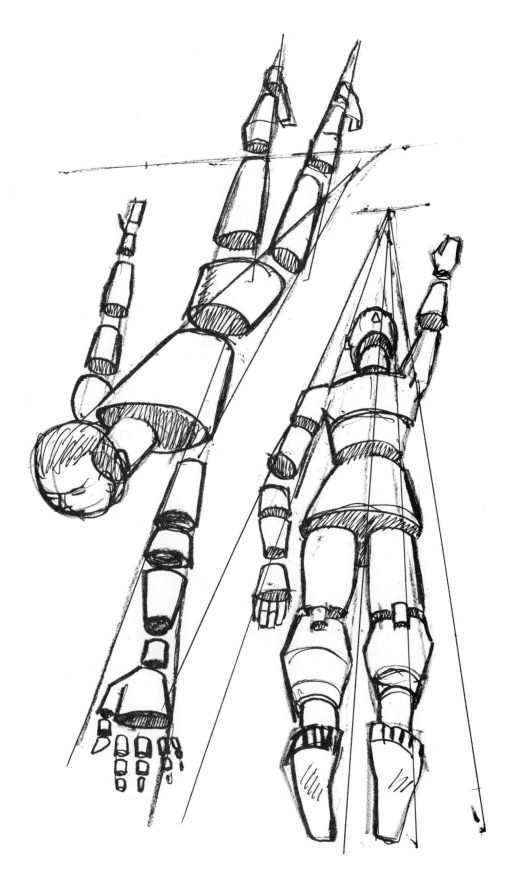

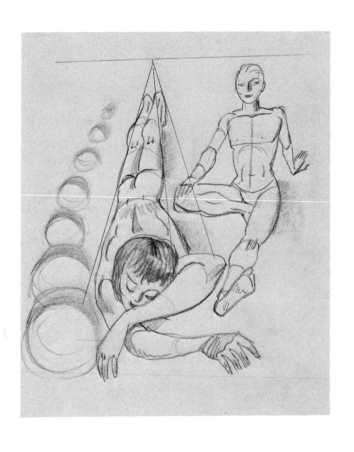

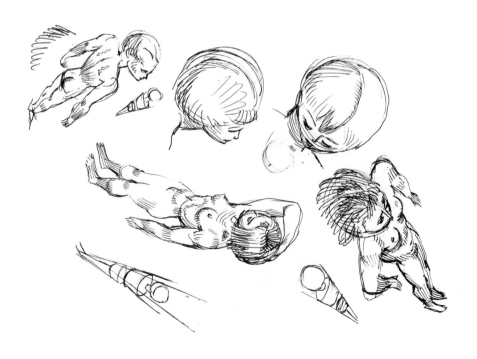

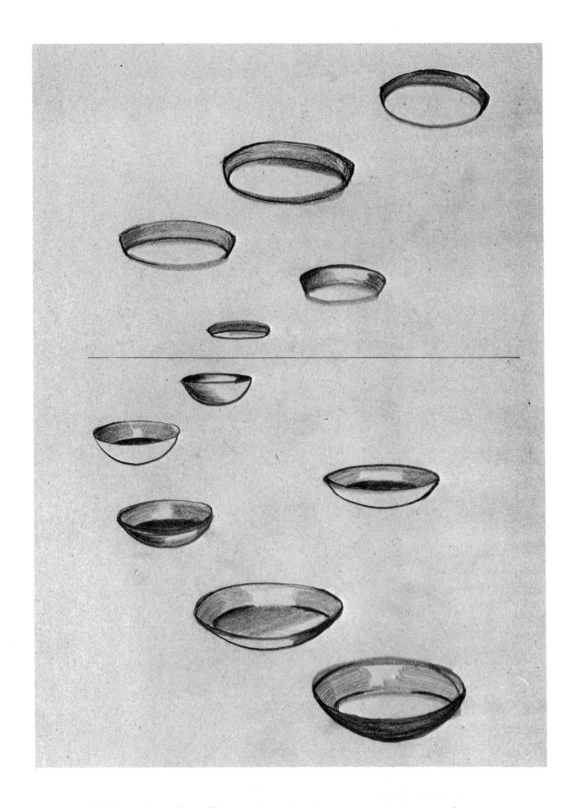

Notice that the ellipses seem to become narrower and narrower as they approach the eye level of the viewer, either from below or from above.

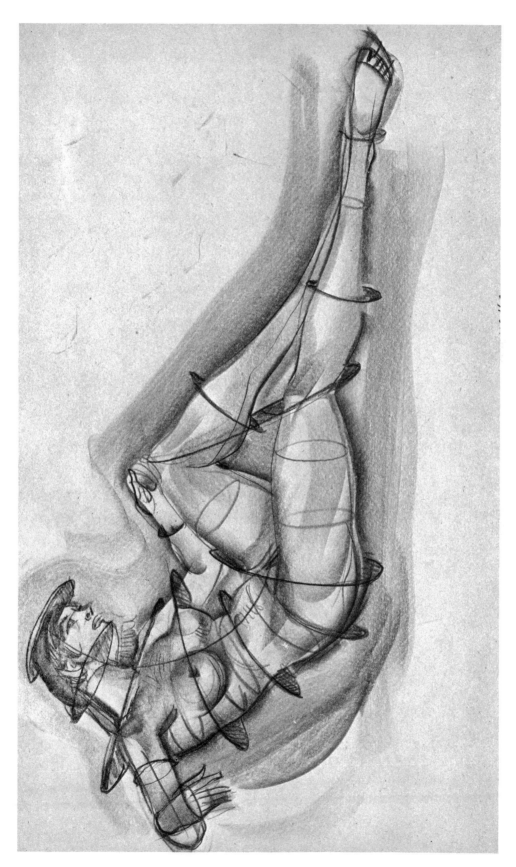

PROPORTIONS

It is a general custom among students to gauge proportion by the use of the head as a unit of size comparison. The conventional ideal figure is about eight heads tall (including the figure's own head, of course).

This does not mean that all people are equally proportioned and that the eight-head-high figure should be an absolute guide. The variations are great. For instance, an ideal proportion of a well-built man would be three vertically placed heads wide at the shoulders. Although there are few men eight heads high and three heads wide at the shoulders, use such general proportions as a key to the ideal figure and make your adjustments to suit the individual type to be drawn.

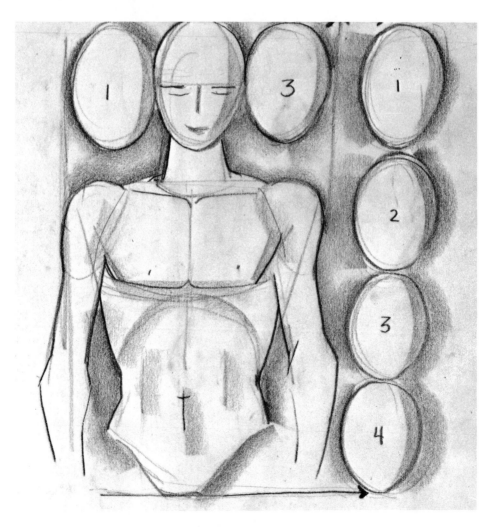

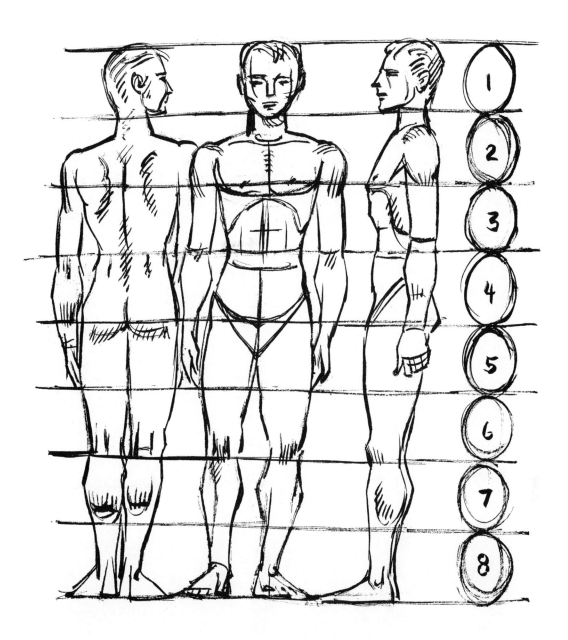

EGG SHAPE

The egg shape is a generalization of the whole head form. There are, of course, many variations. Scientists classify the two major head types under the names *brachycephalic*—short-headed and wide—and *dolichocephalic*—long-headed and narrow. Within these two major classifications are innumerable variations.

Let us, however, study the generalized head shape and the basic nature of the shape of features.

THE NECK

A strong, circular column sturdily supports the head upon the shoulders. It has, within its simple external structure, the capability of graceful and subtle movements, allowing the head to turn, to incline in many directions, and to aid in the expression of many moods.

The first concern in drawing the neck must be to learn the basic setting and proportions of the neck in relation to the head and torso.

The many veins and tendons, muscles, and subsurface parts that show in the neck form must not disturb too drastically the basic column.

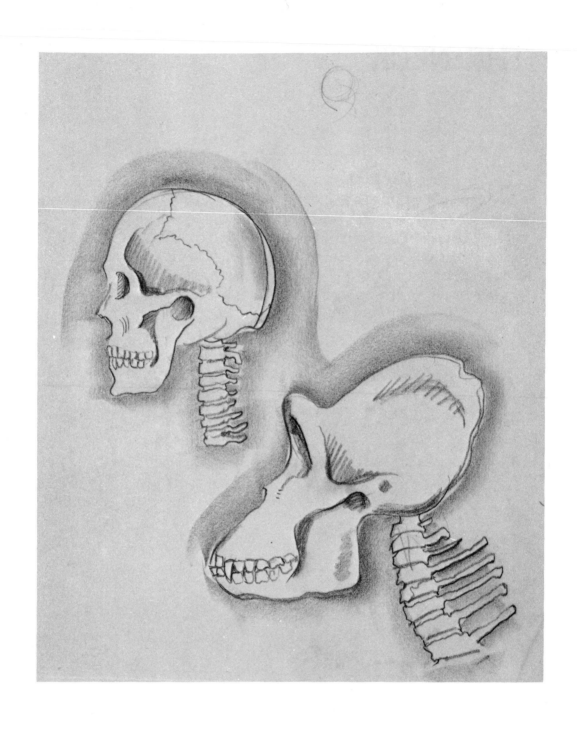

FEATURES

There are billions of people in the world, but no two are identical in appearance. No two faces in the world are exactly the same. This curious fact is true, despite the relatively similar character of the head structure and the same general shape of the features.

Here we shall examine the basic forms and shapes of features of which the external head and features are composed, but it is suggested that the student, throughout his life as an artist, never cease to examine the living faces about him—as well as his own—and find the subtle differences in form, character, and expression that account for this extraordinary variety.

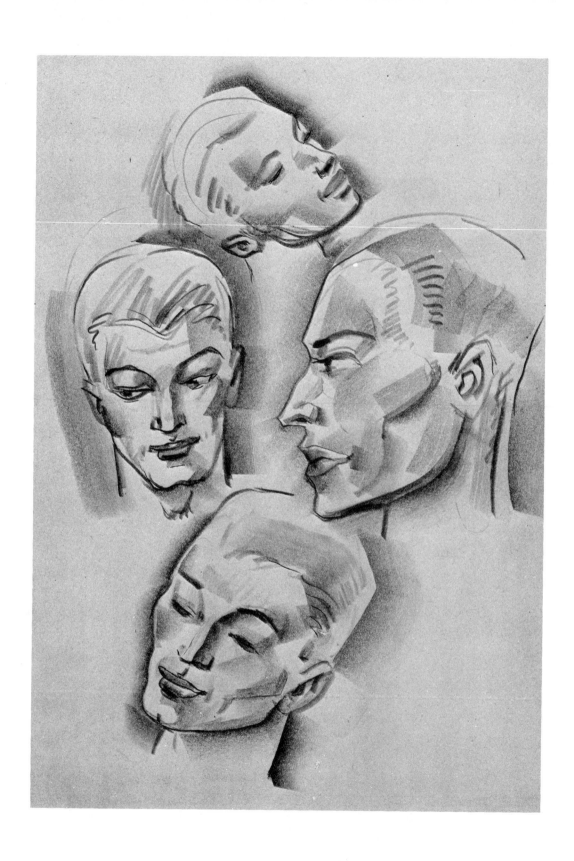

THE NOSE

The wedge-shaped form is a generalization of the typical nose. The variations, as we know, are numberless, but the use of this structural geometric form will allow for the application of variations to a sound base.

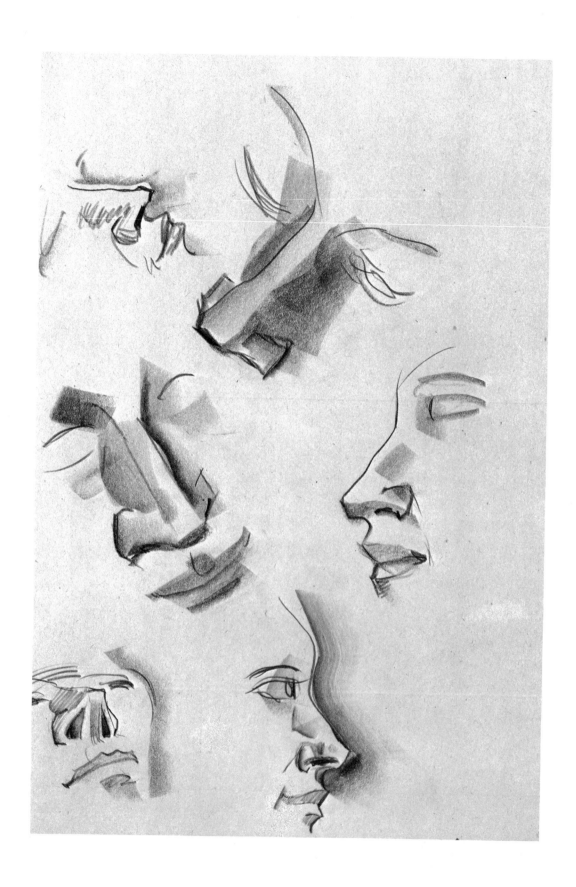

THE EYE

The eye, complicated as it is, does not present a very complex problem for the artist.

Just as the other features and the whole body have been reduced to a few essential geometric forms, the eye is shown here in its essential division of shapes.

Study them and study and sketch your own eyes with the object of capturing the "living eyes" as you see them in the faces of people you meet. You do not see the details but rather the total, vital orb.

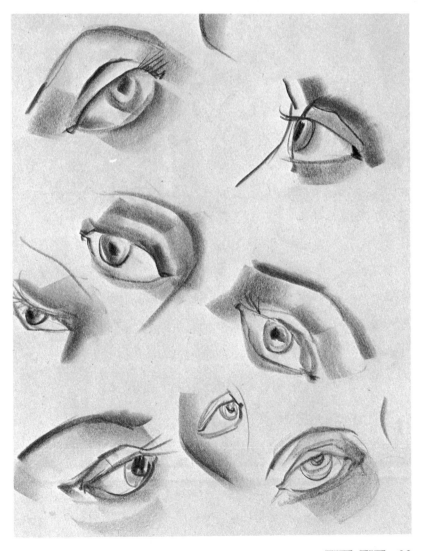

THE MOUTH

The mouth is extremely mobile and changes its character in many ways according to changes of mood and speech. When drawing such a change-able object you must search for the mood expressed and stress that quality.

The basic lip formations shown here will help establish the general character of the mouth, from which you will make your departures in search of the "speaking," expressive mouth.

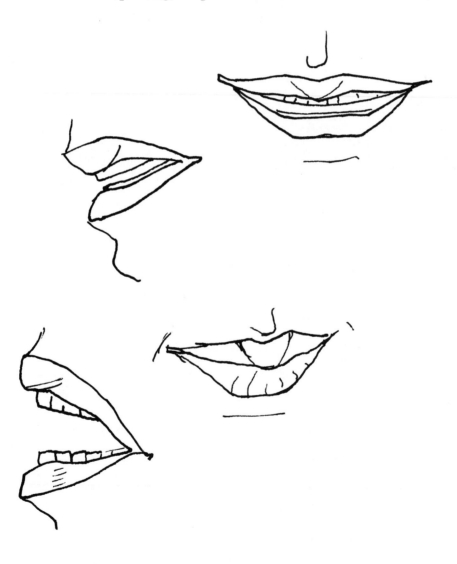

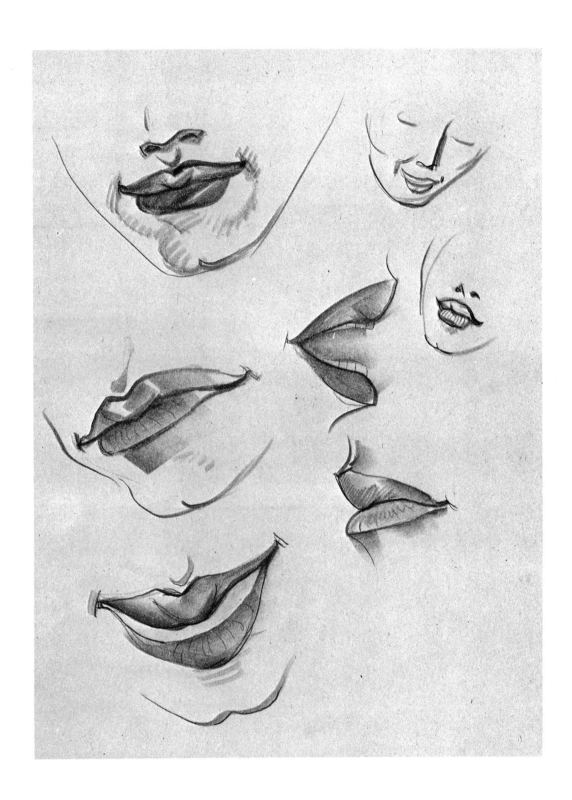

THE EAR

The intricate convolutions in the ear forms may seem difficult to draw at the outset. Upon close examination, the ear is an odd-shaped, abstract-looking organ. However, for most drawing needs, the ear may be drawn in similar fashion to those models shown here.

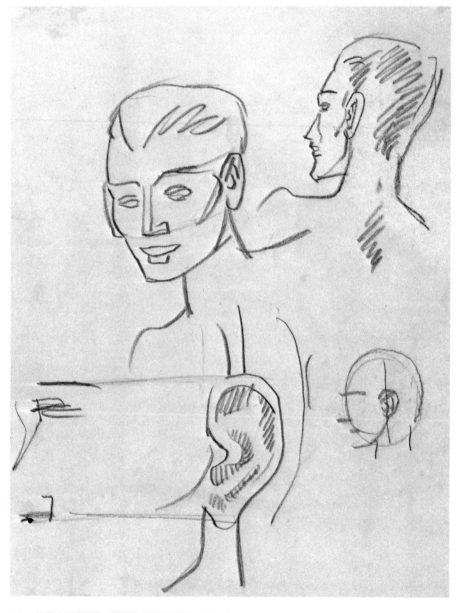

HANDS

The wonderful instruments called hands are at once subtle and simple to draw. The elaborate anatomy of hands may be reduced to the few basic forms demonstrated here. It is of value to learn this process of basic construction. With it, hands may be drawn performing any function and in any position.

Once you have become adept at drawing these elemental hands you may begin to add the subtlety and grace, the power and dexterity, and all the beautiful, intensely expressive gestures of which hands are capable.

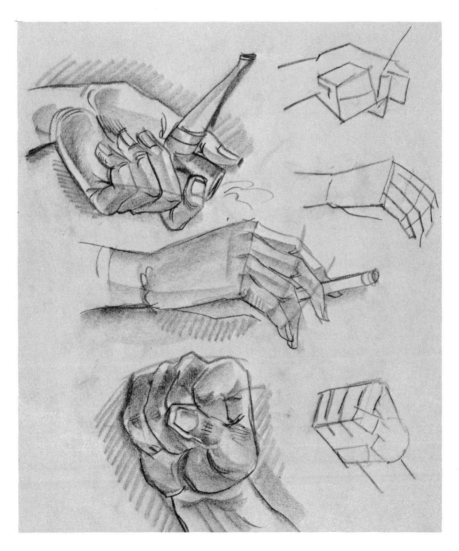

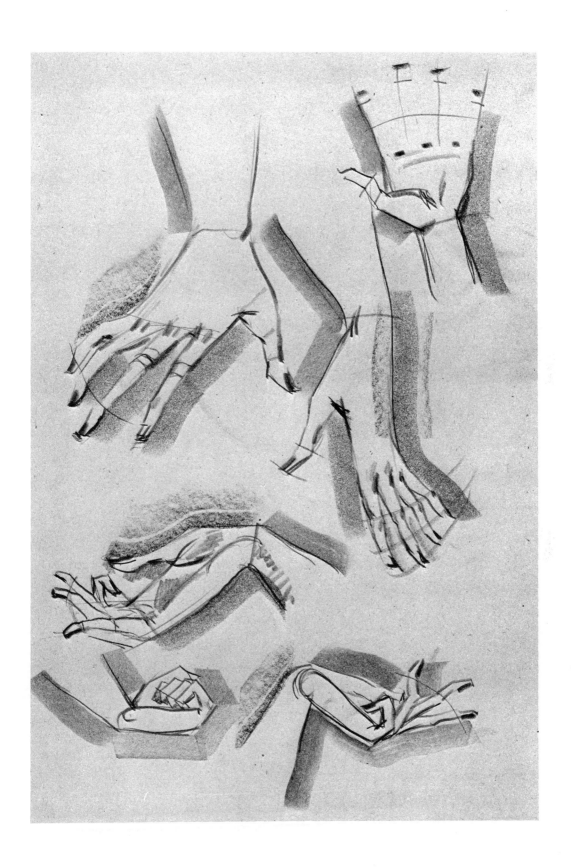

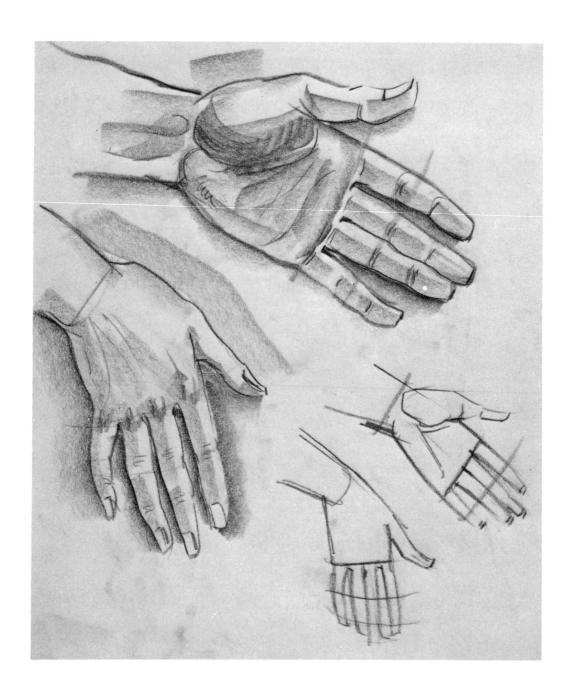

Hands speak a rich language and the artist should be able to transfer that language to his drawing. But—such subtleties only follow after the ability to draw strong, simple understructures.

Study these hands, which are reduced to a few geometric forms. Draw them in every position shown here, pose your own hands in other positions, and draw them in the same simple terms. When you have practiced such hand drawing until you are proficient, begin to refine your drawings of hands and make them live.

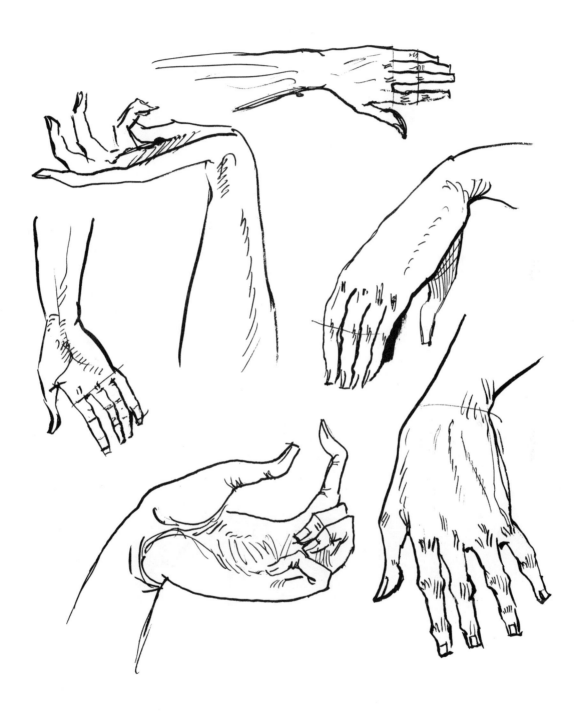

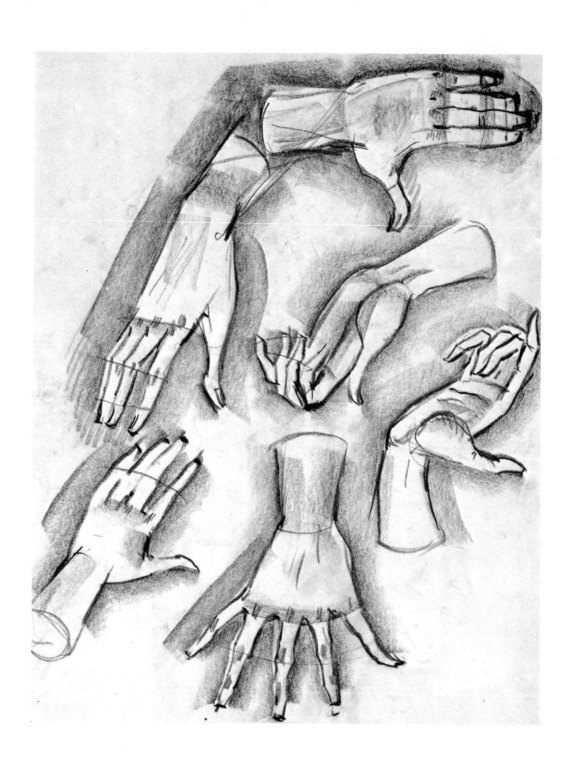

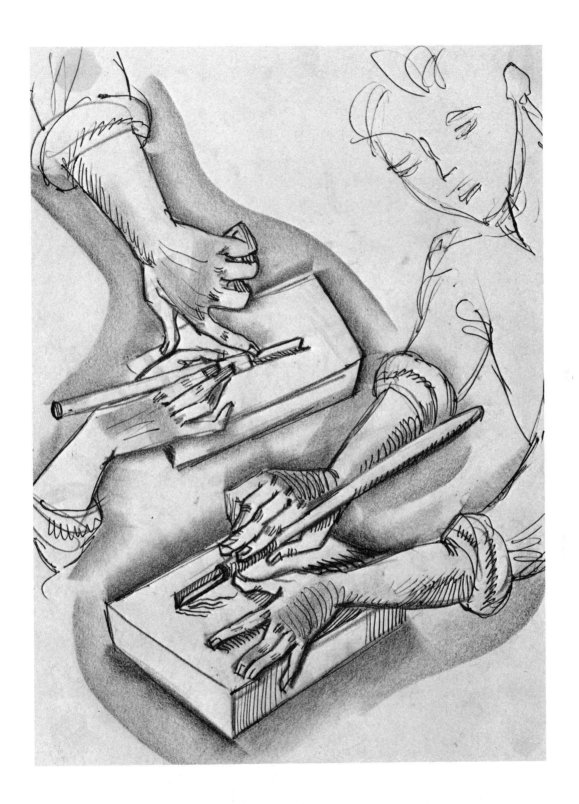

THE ARM

The arm is an indispensable tool capable of complex articulation at its three joint areas. It has the potential of exerting great power and speed as well as subtle and beautiful, expressive and rhythmic movements.

Here you will find the basic structural forms of the arm—first reduced to the essential geometric shapes and then, superimposed on these few forms, the important curves and protuberances made by muscle and bone anatomy close to the surface.

In keeping with the thesis of this book—that is, that the vastly complex anatomy of the body should be seen from the artist's viewpoint and not from that of the dissecting anatomist—the following examples of drawing the arm are simplified. They are drawn in various positions demonstrating their action possibilities, with all details subordinated to that end.

The single, long bone in the upper arm called the humerus acts, as far as the artist is concerned, as the armature does in clay sculpture. It makes no surface protuberance. It is deeply embedded in muscle. The heavy deltoid muscle caps the shoulder in the same manner as an epaulet. The biceps muscles, strongly bulging when the arm is bent, along with the triceps on the back of the upper arm, are the forms to be stressed in drawing a powerful man's arm.

In the forearm the two bones, the ulna and the radius, unite with the humerus at the elbow, and, while they are well covered with muscle at the upper forearm, they come close to the surface as they approach the wrist joint.

These muscles and joints are less pronounced in the female arm but of course they are there, less hard and knotty in character, and curving gracefully and smoothly.

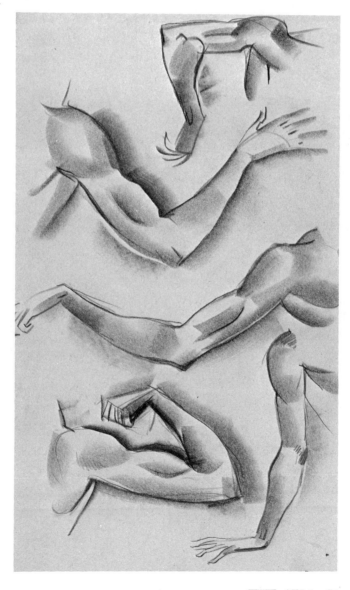

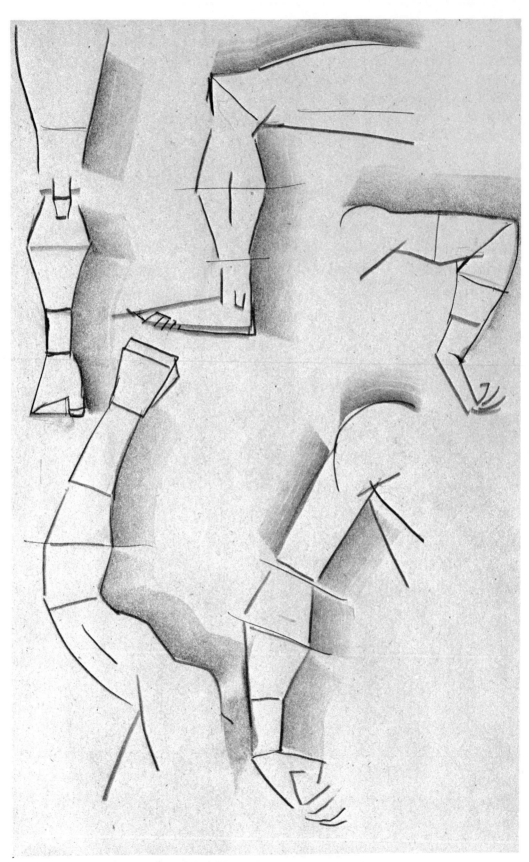

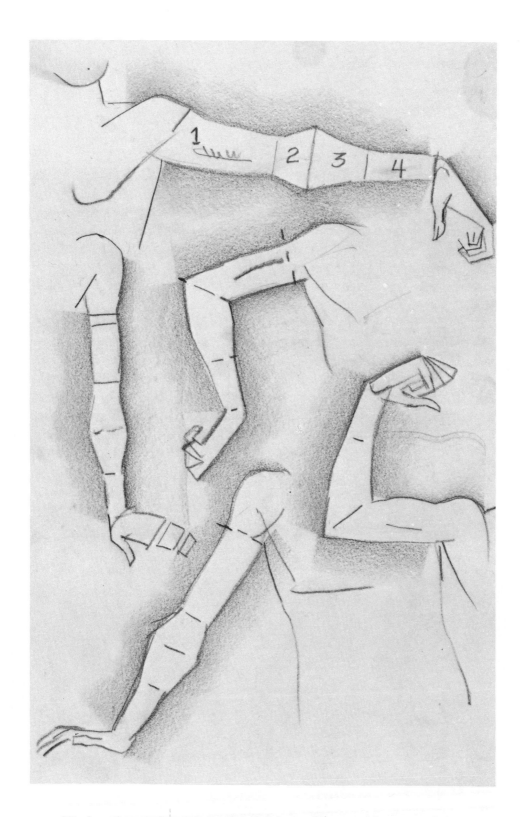

Notice the main geometric divisions that are the essential forms into which the arm may be divided for drawing purposes. These divisions pertain no matter what position the arm assumes.

THE LEG

The long, strong bone of the upper leg, or thigh, is called the femur. It makes no surface appearance. The main muscle is the long one at the back of the thigh, called the biceps of the leg, and is quite prominent.

In the lower leg are two bones, the tibia and the fibula. The tibia lies close to the skin surface, forming the hard shin area from knee to ankle. The tibia joins the femur at the knee. At the knee is the patella bone, or kneecap, shaped like a little rounded cap. Two large muscles form the bulge of the calf.

Again, for our purposes, the leg has been reduced to a few simple large divisions, geometric in shape. Many refinements of drawing may be added to these simplifications. The variations in character of muscular development, from the powerful male leg to the smooth flow of a well-shaped female leg, do not depart too drastically from these basic shapes. When your first drawings are based upon those geometric shapes the details will fall into their proper place.

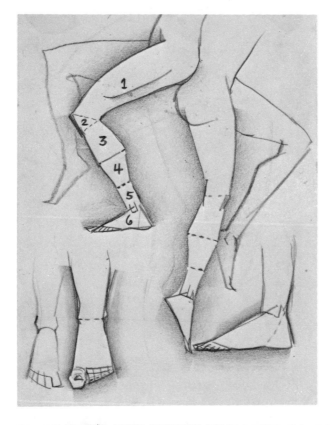

THE FOOT

The foot is, in essence, a triangle when seen in profile. As it turns from that position in relation to your eye, its form becomes a variation of that geometric form.

Study the many different positions shown here, and draw your own feet for the study of greater detail.

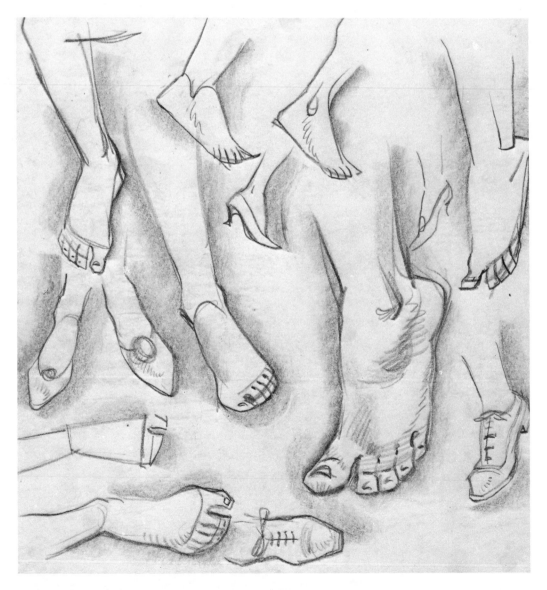

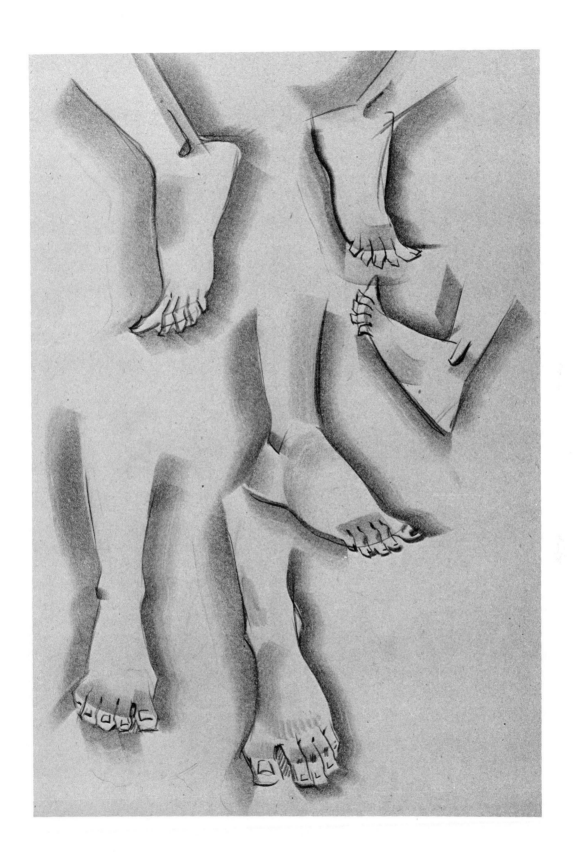

HOW TO USE THESE FIGURE STUDIES

During your study of these figure drawings utilize them in the following ways.

1. Study the stages demonstrating how the pose and basic structure were first indicated in as few lines as possible. Keep a sketch pad beside you and try to make simple working-drawing analyses in similar fashion. Your work need not look exactly the same nor even use exactly the same approach, but the same purpose should be kept in mind, that of making a simple, basic scaffold upon which you can add refining details with the assurance that the nature of the pose is caught and that the proportions are reasonably correct. Keep your structural lines light so that they will disappear in the "finished" drawing. (Those shown here are excessively dark for proper reproduction in this book.)

2. Notice the effort to "summarize" rather than to reproduce the details of the figure. It is not your function to manufacture small human beings on paper but rather to symbolize them.

   These figure drawings are my concept and viewpoint of the models. I have neither the skill nor the desire to simulate humans precisely, my purpose is to "tell about them." For that reason and an even better one, the preservation of your own style and viewpoint, do not copy the finished drawings. Study what is informative in them: how contours and details are reduced to essentials, how planes and forms are suggested by means of geometry and light and shade. The techniques of application of pencil or crayon or pen in the drawings should only concern you when they serve as aids to the development of your own style.

Most important, the use of these figures in the above ways will serve as practice for you. Draw each figure repeatedly and in the course of so doing you will develop a familiarity with the proportions and action possibilities of the figure and also dexterity in the use of your materials.

THE MALE FIGURE

The strong, well-defined forms of the male figure, with fewer fleshy curves than those in the female figure, make for a more direct examination of basic structure, accompanied by fewer aesthetic and emotional distractions. The essential architectonic structure is more easily traceable.

The well-developed male figure of good proportions has relatively square shoulders, wider than those of the female. The long form of the torso tapers to the waist, and the hips are narrower than those of an average well-shaped female. The thighs are long and narrow, tapering to the knee.

The muscles of the male are much more developed than those of the female, but except in the case of deliberate development for athletic purposes, or through hard manual labor, they do not bulge greatly from the smooth geometric shapes into which we have divided the figure.

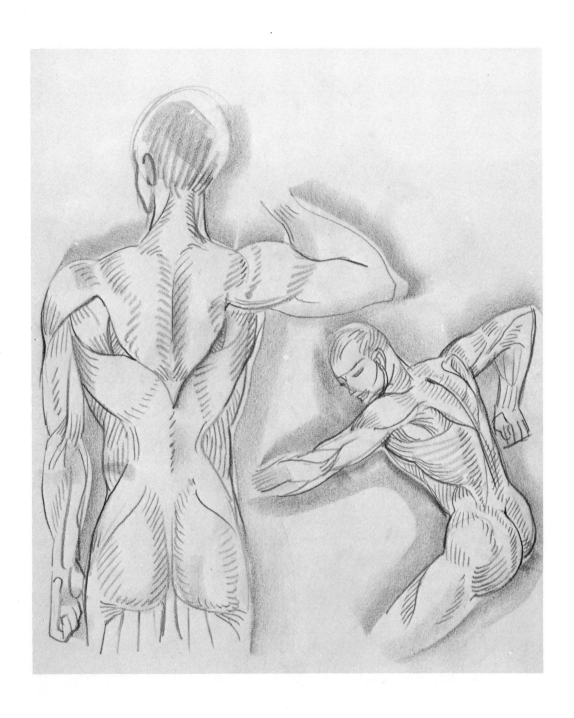

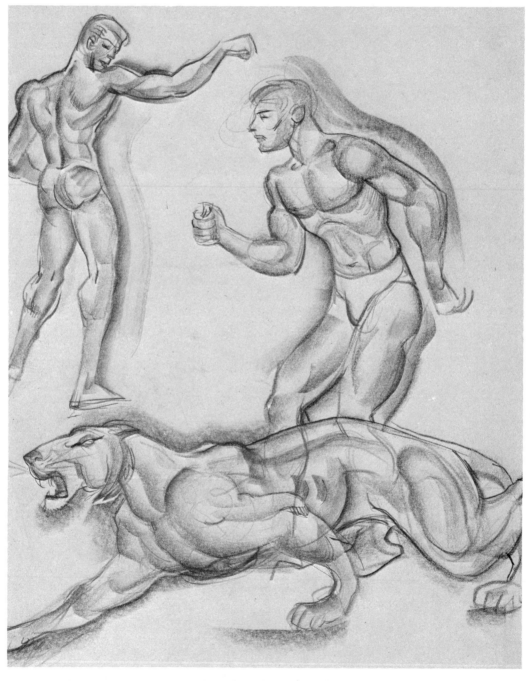

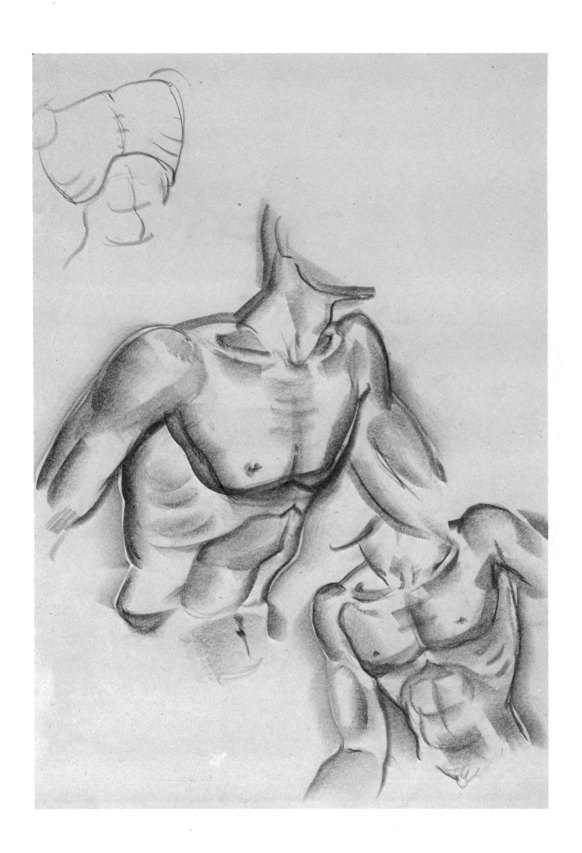

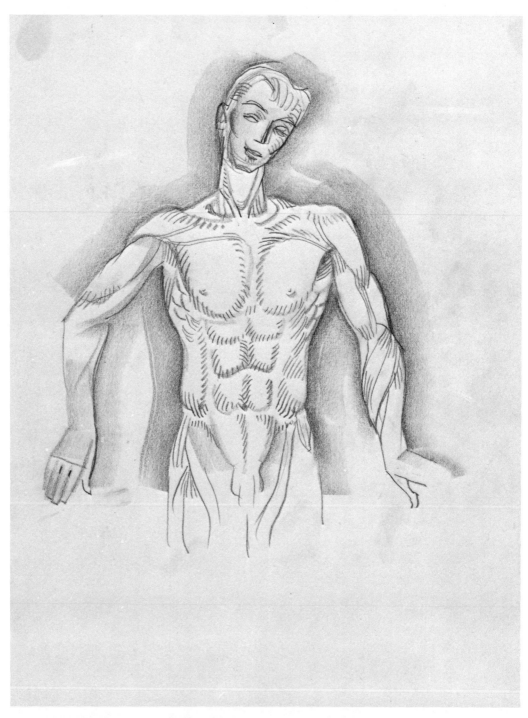

THE FEMALE FIGURE

The female figure has been the preoccupation of artists throughout the ages, and each artist has expressed its beauty and grace in his own manner, dictated by his emotional responses.

No art teacher can hope to teach the student how to look upon "woman" and how to depict that subtle, changeable creature. I shall certainly not attempt to do so here.

What we shall do is work together on the process of drawing a reasonable facsimile of the female form. When you have learned this, you may then add all your emotional responses with the assurance that you are doing so on the basis of a proportionate, presentable prototype of a female figure.

Your "finished" drawings will not look like mine, but the use of the drawing approaches that I have found satisfactory should help you to draw a sound generalization of a female.

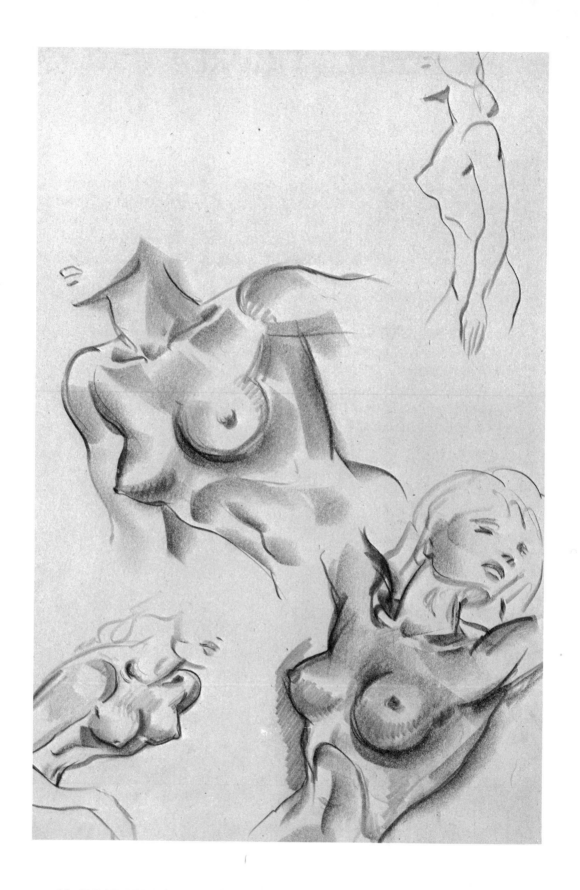

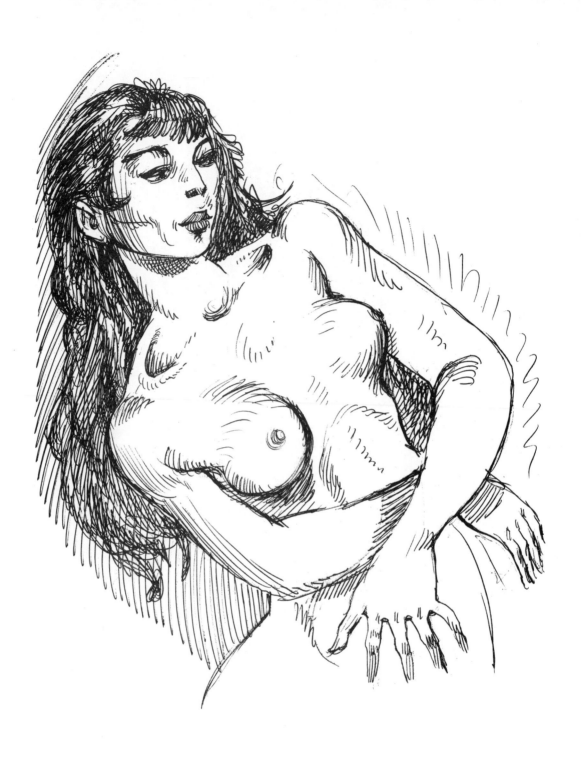

LIGHT AND SHADE

There are a number of reasons for the interest of artists in the nature of light and shadow that make intense study of the subject valid for the art student. The obvious, practical reasons are the following:

1. The use of shading on the figure helps in large part to simulate the third dimension in a drawing on the two-dimensional paper by suggesting roundness or bulk to the forms of the figure.

2. Shading is an aid in achieving "realism" since nothing in nature exists that is unaffected by either natural sources of light or by man-made illumination.

3. Light and shade in a drawing can be used to express distance. Objects or figures in the foreground are darker than those in the distance. Highlights are brighter close to the eye than farther away.

There are in addition to these functional qualities other artistic contributions to a drawing through the use of light and shade. The bold truths of a working drawing by a draftsman and the renderings of architects or engineers are dictated by an obvious need to be as explicit as possible and to leave nothing to the imagination. The artist, however, works hand in hand with the imagination of the beholder of his works. He implies and suggests that his works are symbols rather than reproductions. His communication is not a blueprint but rather an invitation to share a subtle experience. That is the function and much-to-be-hoped-for accomplishment of a work of art.

The use of light and shade by good artists enters into art expression in much the same manner as the use of color. The artist must use it to contrast, balance, and help the movement of his composition and give a sense of play and vitality as well as to help supply the "air" in which the drawing lives and breathes.

With these aims in mind the artist is under no compulsion to be exact in his application of light and shade. Just as it is permissible for him to exaggerate proportions or forms where they serve his artistic purpose, so he may accentuate and intensify or unrealistically subdue or eliminate lights and tones where they aid his creative statement.

It is well to discover the source of light that falls on a figure when you draw it and to determine the value of the shadows thrown or forms blocked from that light. But the main consideration is the total statement of the artist, and he should bear in mind at all times that the lighting of his drawing must serve to intensify the mood or beautify the object.

Study the basic nature of light and shade. Observe the character of shadows cast and gradations from bright light to deep shading on forms in relation to the source of light. Use the knowledge so gained to help you in drawing solid forms, but avoid carrying your shading to the point where realism goes beyond the artistic and the charm goes out of your drawing.

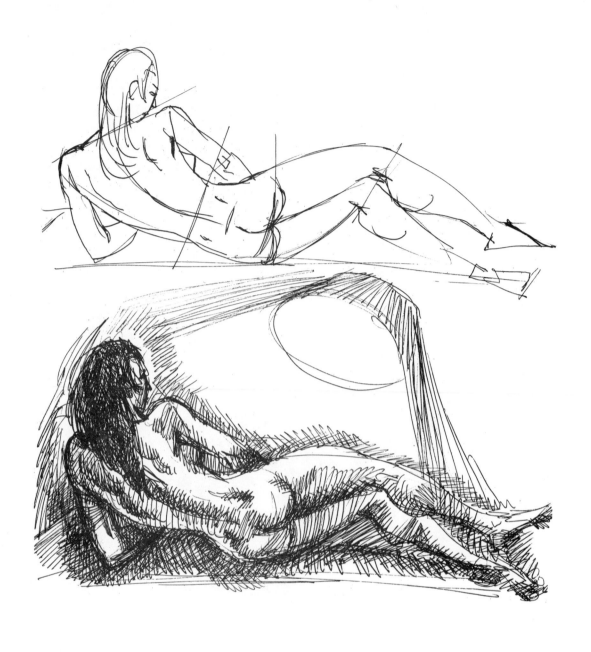

ACTION

An artist is rarely submissive to strict rules of procedure. The very essence of his profession, that of creation, must of necessity violate rules laid down by other men.

The methods of seeing and analyzing action, and the first swift lines applied to the paper in capturing that action, are not the only approach possible, but I have found them satisfactory as an aid in arriving at an understanding of the intention of the pose assumed by the model, a quick analysis of the larger movements involved, and a generalization of the proportions.

The same simple approach may be used in "invented" figures, though ease in drawing action figures in similar detail comes with considerable practice.

In studying these plates you may find that the same procedures of first steps are not followed. This occurs for two reasons. One is that the complexity of the pose will not allow for the same simple guidelines used in less subtle situations. The second reason for the variation is that I, too, do not wish to be bound by a rigid procedure, and my first approach to the drawing differs in some details. However, the search for the most direct, simplified statement of the nature of an action prevails throughout these studies, even though there are these variations.

Try to use similar direct and simple analytical approaches.

DIRECTION LINES

Here are some fluid action drawings accompanied by a series of analytical line drawings.

Some artists, when they are making quick sketches of the posed model or spontaneous notes of action, use this "direction line" approach. With a few swift lines the action is caught, and the drawing of structure will fall into place along those action guidelines.

As an aid in acquiring a fluent line suitable for drawing action, the student should form the habit of mentally performing the action to be drawn. Some artists even get up from their drawing boards and perform the action physically, follow-through and all.

This habit as well as the all-important one of careful observation of actions performed by people all around you will remove the objectionable quality of arrested action, the static quality so prevalent in action photographs.

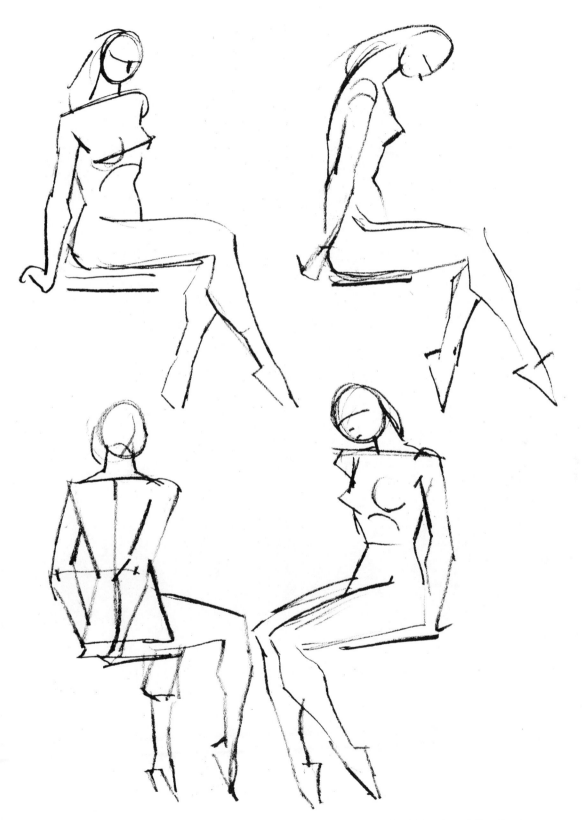

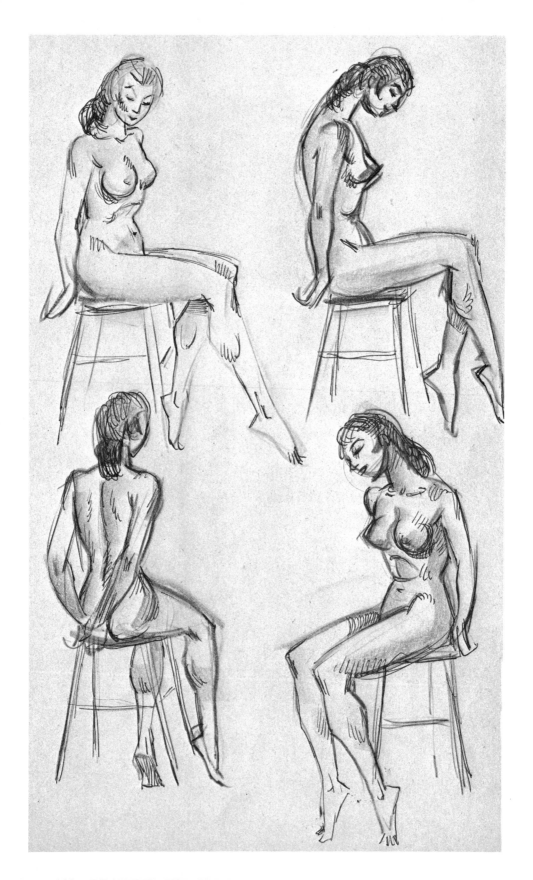

REPOSE

A figure in repose is never, even during sleep, without some muscular tensions. We cannot attain the almost completely collapsed appearance of the cat when we are at rest. The firmness of our bones and the relatively tight-skinned compactness of our bodies prevent any great change in the appearance of our bodies when we recline.

To draw a figure in repose convincingly we must find all the points of support contact and stress these in our drawings. Whenever the pull of gravity is visible in a reclining figure it must be accentuated.

Always remember that, as an artist, yours is the right to tell the story of an action or the character of repose by methods allowing for exaggeration.

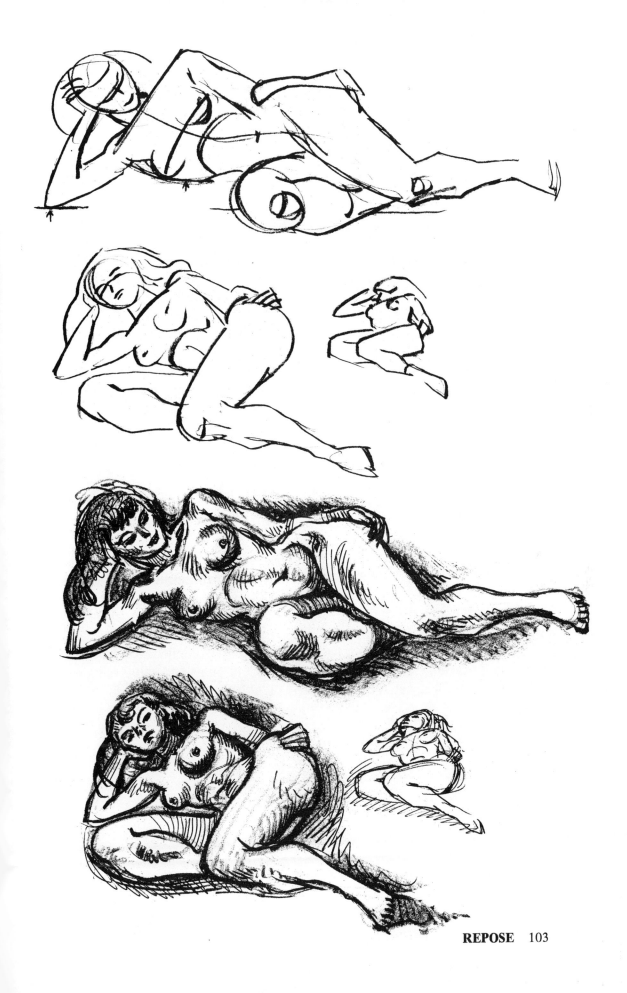

INFLUENCE AND TECHNIQUES

Either you have already decided you intend to be an artist or you are testing your abilities and want help in developing them. In any event you are thinking in terms of art and therefore you must, at the outset, develop a special point of view—one that is essential for the artist or student.

You must be yourself.

That may sound like an unnecessary admonition since it is impossible to be anyone other than yourself. You are you, so what is the problem? The sad fact is that despite the difficulty of forging anyone else's handwriting, in art or script, thousands of art students try to emulate the work of artists whom they admire—to the destruction of their own individuality.

Influence has very valid qualities for the student. Admiration for the work of great artists and understanding of their high motives can contribute to the student's excitement, inspiration, and knowledge. Much of a technical nature may be learned from the study of great paintings. A fine artist as a teacher may enrich the understanding and skill of the student. But—and this must not be forgotten—every fine painter painted in his own manner, made his own statements drawn from his own visions, emotions, and driving forces within him.

You must at no point in your studies or career acquire anyone else's style, dream anyone else's dreams, or say anything in paint that is not your own statement.

Having said this, I hasten to add that the art student, as a most important adjunct to his studies, must go to art museums and exhibitions and look at the fine art reproductions available in books as much as possible.

LINE

Here are two drawings showing different uses of line.

The drawing on the left is done with an even pressure line throughout.

The drawing on the right was done with line of varying thickness, with the result of creating an impression of three-dimensional form.

Each artist eventually evolves his own handwriting in line drawing.

DRAWING IN LINE

No such concept as pure line exists in nature. Everything in nature is three dimensional. A slim blade of grass has bulk, a strand of hair is round. Line, like perspective and foreshortening, is a visual rationale, a symbol of truth, not the truth itself.

Line drawing has elements of artistic expression, possibilities quite different from solid drawing that concentrates on portraying three-dimensional bulk through the use of shading.

Line, a creation of man in itself, is a truly creative medium in the hands of a sensitive artist. When the line used in drawing is even and unaccented throughout it is still capable of suggesting interior forms while retaining a beauty and power of its own. When used in irregular thicknesses or broken continuity it is a highly emotional art medium.

The curious quality of line as a drawing method is that while it is a highly sophisticated art tool in the hands of a sensitive artist, it is the method employed by children in their first efforts to draw the objects about them. They have not yet learned to "see" the thing around the corner—the knowledge of the third dimension. They indicate the "border lines" of the object and are content that they have told the story sufficiently. And so they have, very often. For us, too, line can very often tell our drawing story effectively and sufficiently.

MODELS

No matter how far you live from a life class or art school or from where you can hire a professional model you always have one patient and sympathetic model available—yourself. It is not important that you be shaped like a Greek god or goddess.

Draw your own hands and feet in many positions. Use a mirror to help when necessary. Draw your features—not with the purpose of catching a likeness but for study purposes. No hired model will give you such opportunity for close study and such a range of poses as you can get with an enlarging mirror of the type sold for shaving and make-up.

If it is possible for you to draw from posed models other than yourself, you cannot get too much of it for your studies. Most of the artists I know, long-time "professionals," are delighted to join a life-sketching group whenever possible.

The best poses for study purposes are of five or ten minutes in length. Some teachers prefer to have the model pose for two or three minutes. The value of these short poses is to train the student to seek out the salient character of the pose, the main proportions, and the important shadows and lights, thereby learning to eliminate the relatively non-essential details.

There are occasions when a long study of a pose is desirable but, even so, very few poses remain exactly the same in either their action or lighting over a long period of time. When such detail study of the figure is required photographs and casts will better serve your purpose.

Here we have a series of studies made from photographs of sculpture and from casts and sculptured figures.

DRAWING FROM CASTS

The obvious value for the student in drawing from casts of sculpture is that the models remain unmoving in their pose and careful study is possible. Another value is the fact that white plaster casts allow for study of *true* light and shade, which is not the case in drawing from life. The live model has local pigmentation of varying degrees of light and dark values that are hard to separate from the lights and darks produced by the source of illumination.

A third value for the artist is the most important and most pleasurable one. That is the ideal proportions and ready-made simplification to be learned from the classic statues of antiquity and from some of the great Renaissance sculpture.

When casts are not available, modern photography has given us splendid, sharply detailed photographs of great figure sculpture that will serve almost the same purpose.

The series of examples of cast drawing shown here will bear out the fact that they are excellent sources of study of the figure. We have used photographs of antique sculpture, chosen for their essential simplicity. Notice how the sculptor reduced the complex forms of every part of the body to simple planes and smooth forms. Wherever it was necessary the sculptor used the right of the artist to exaggerate or underplay the "natural" to produce the beautiful or the emotional.

I have heard fine musicians, talking in technical terms among themselves, agree that in some of the great, turbulent compositions, the playing of all the exact notes is not indispensable in a dramatic playing of the music. Exactness, in some cases, may distract the artist and make his rendition mechanical, devoid of the intensity of feeling desired.

It is equally true in drawing from these great sculpture pieces. One may not take liberties to the point of changing the nature of the work of art on whim. Rather, it is during the process of searching for the deepest character of the sculpture that the incidentals of detail may be overlooked and even proportions may not be precise.

When you draw from casts or sculptured pieces search for the essential movement and the intended rhythm of the piece as well as the mood.

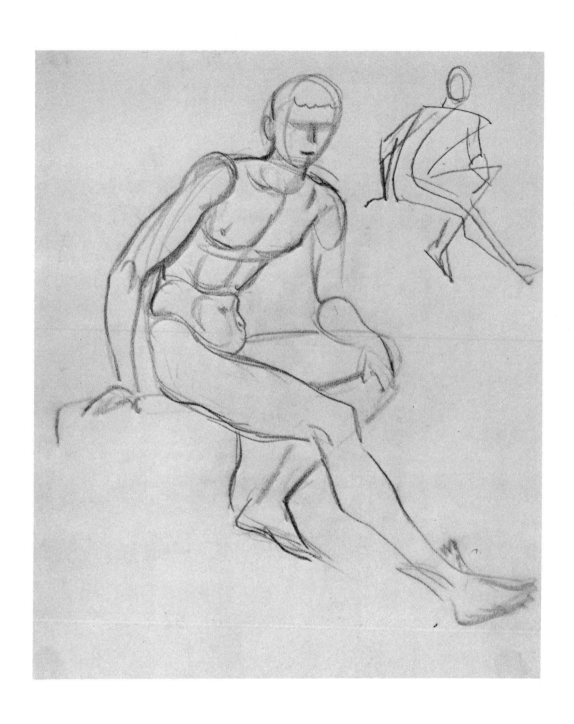

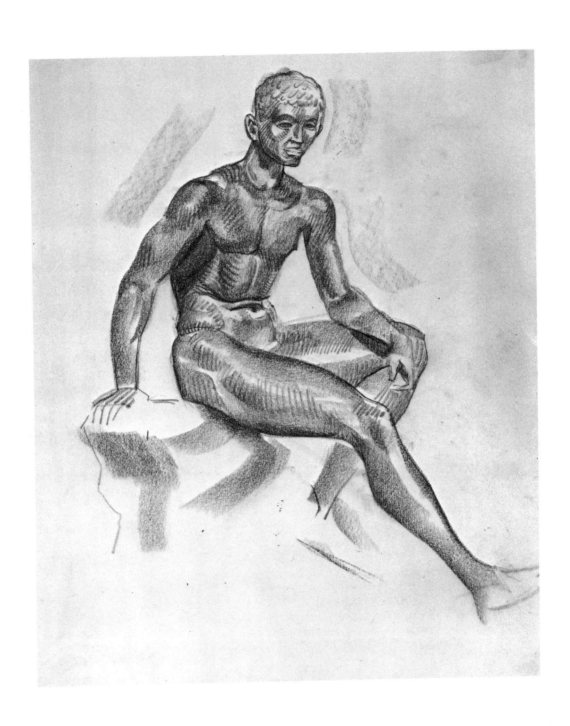

120 **DRAWING THE FIGURE FROM TOP TO TOE**

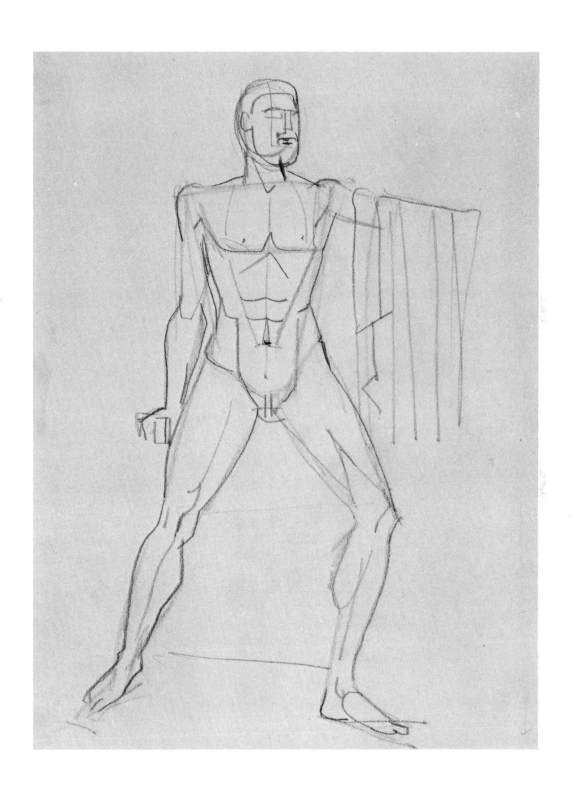

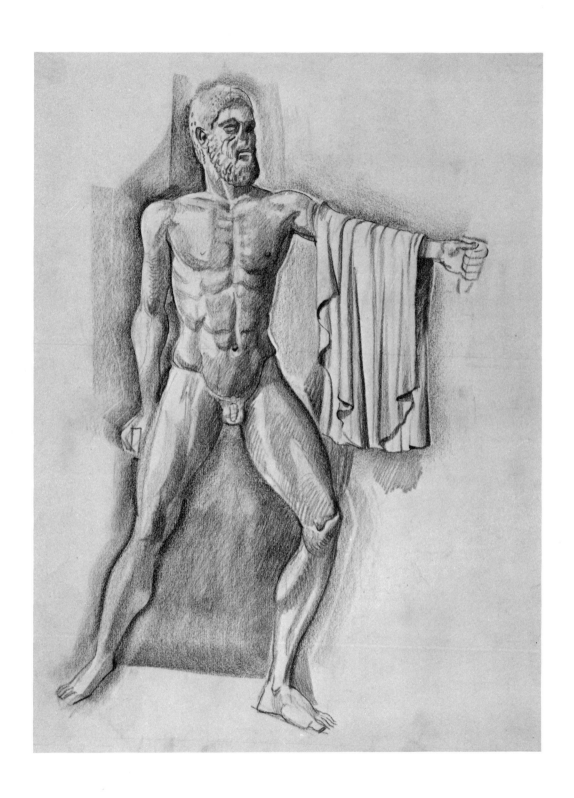

DRAWING THE FIGURE FROM PHOTOGRAPHS

This series of drawings made from the posed model is primarily for instruction in the procedure of examining a pose, analyzing its intent, gauging the general proportions of the figure and application of light and shade, and using various techniques and media of artistic expression.

For such study purposes photographs are a valid aid and I recommend their use. Certainly when live models are not available photographs are of definite value as a substitute. However, I should like to make it clear that a photograph is never a valid replacement for life. To unthinking people the invention of the camera presaged the passing into relative obscurity of the drawing and painting processes. Obviously that did not happen and the happy truth is that never in all history has there been such an intense interest in drawings and paintings by an avid, informed public, and there have never before been so may practicing painters.

There is a simple reason why a photograph cannot replace the living model as a source of more than the basic studies outlined in the first paragraph. The model is breathing and moving (no matter how slightly) and thinking—in short, going through the same vital procedures as the artist—and this is inevitably communicated to the artist and appears in his work.

Utilize these photographs. Follow the steps in basic structure, capture the implied action and the nature of light and shade conveniently made static for your leisure study. You can locate various parts of the body in relation to one another by using imaginary plumb lines and horizontal point-to-point lines.

But in order to breathe life into your drawings you will have to refer to living beings about you.

Very often the movement of a pose is quite subtle. There is a rhythm, however, and it must be found in order to give life to your drawing.

Outline, very lightly, the shapes of the major shadows on the body and then fill them in, using even tonality. When you locate the darkest areas, stress them. Do not try to get in every little area of shadow.

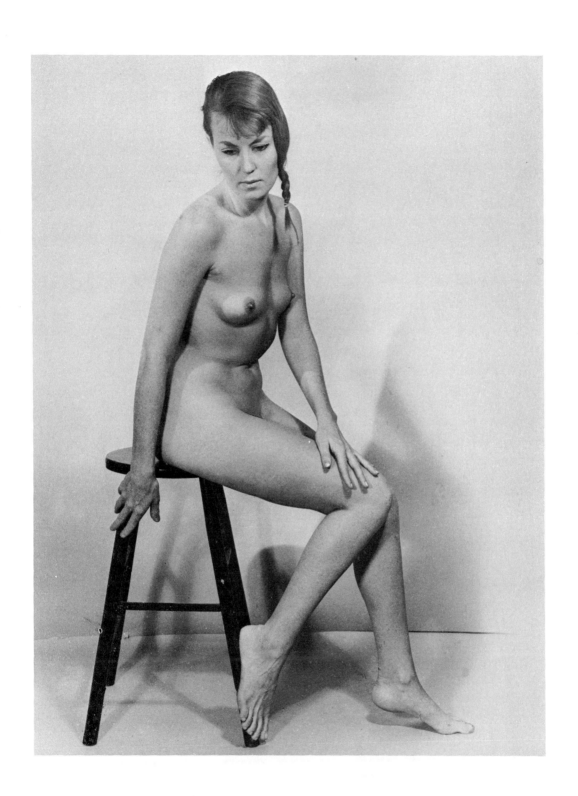

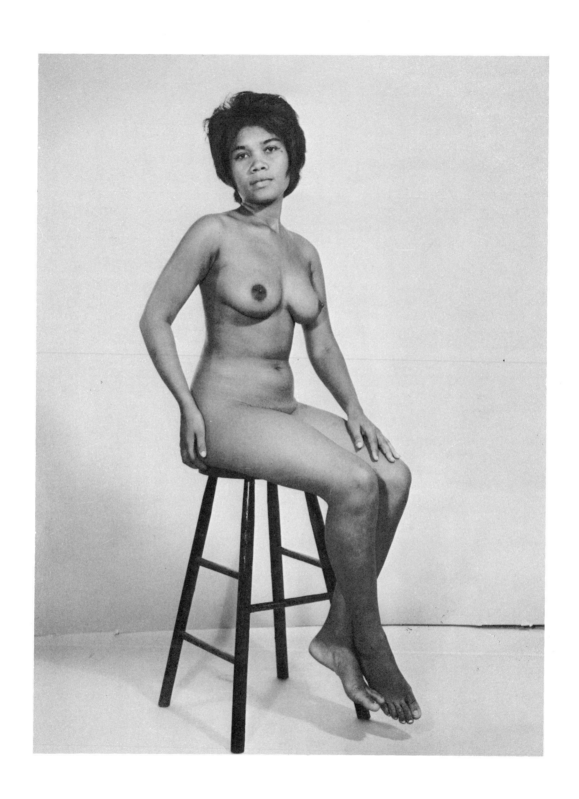

134   **DRAWING THE FIGURE FROM TOP TO TOE**

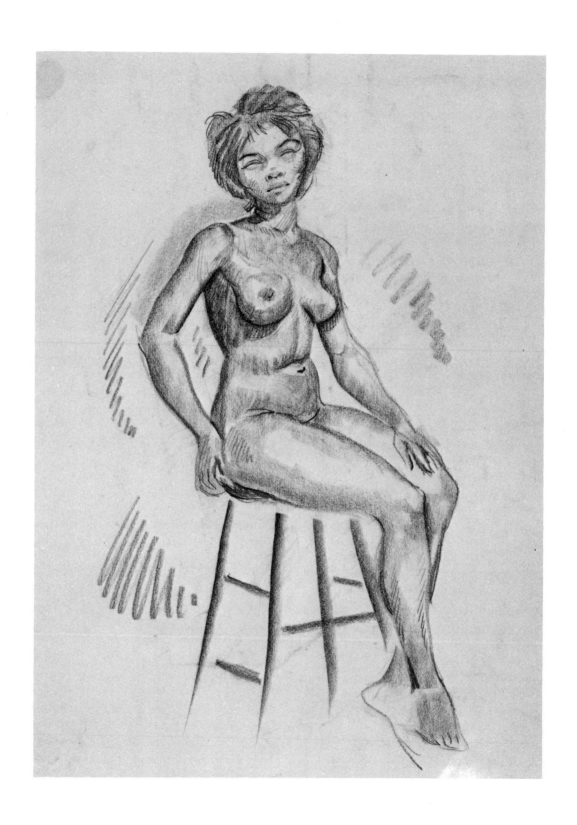

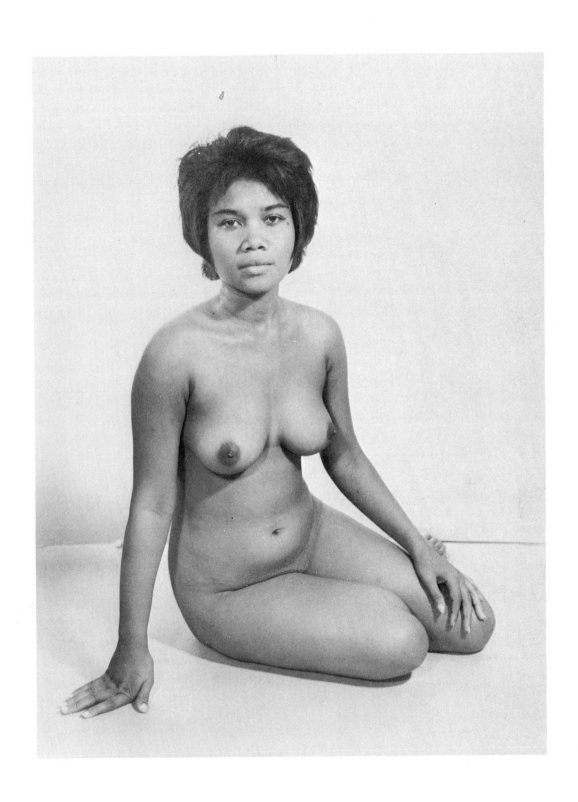

DRAPE OF CLOTHING

The draping of clothing on the figure is directed by three major forces. One is the pull of gravity upon the material. The second is the bulk and movement of the body underneath the clothes. The third is the tensile strength, the firmness of the cloth or built-in folds and shapes of the dress or suit.

These, along with the slight movements caused by air, must be studied in order to draw clothes that "live" with the figure.

Many artists prefer to draw the nude figure in simple detail, and then add the clothing. It seems a plausible approach, considering that it is the normal procedure in life.

Women of the Cages
Bombay

Women of
the Cages
Bombay

Women of the Cages
Bombay

Women of

TEST EXERCISES

This series of "half drawings" will serve as an introduction to a game that is both amusing and instructive.

Finish this bowl of fruit and you will see that the basic geometric forms shown at the beginning of this book (as those which make up the essential character of the human figure) apply in drawing this still life.

Finish the other half of each of these "test exercises," and then go back through the pages of this book and trace *half* of each of a number of the drawings. Finish the untraced half without looking at the book.

You will find the game a challenge and an excellent practice method in acquiring knowledge of the proportions and contours of forms.

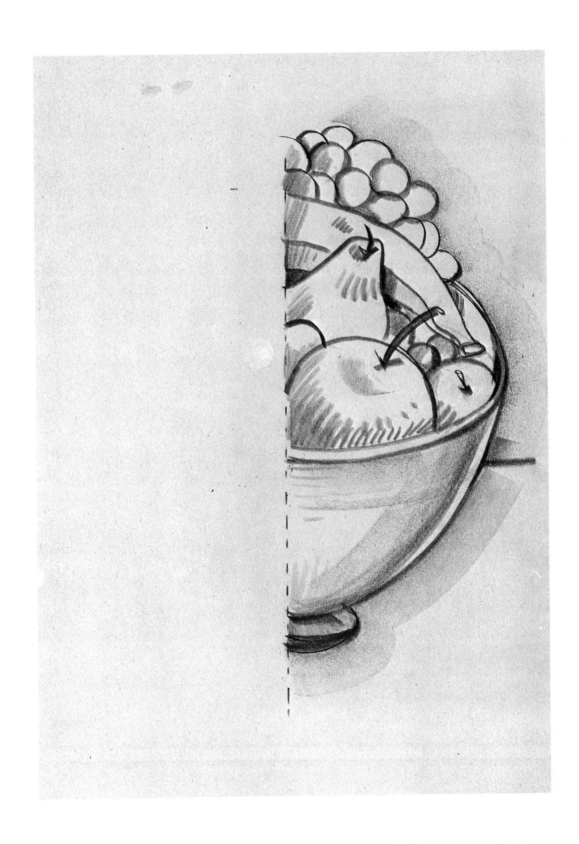

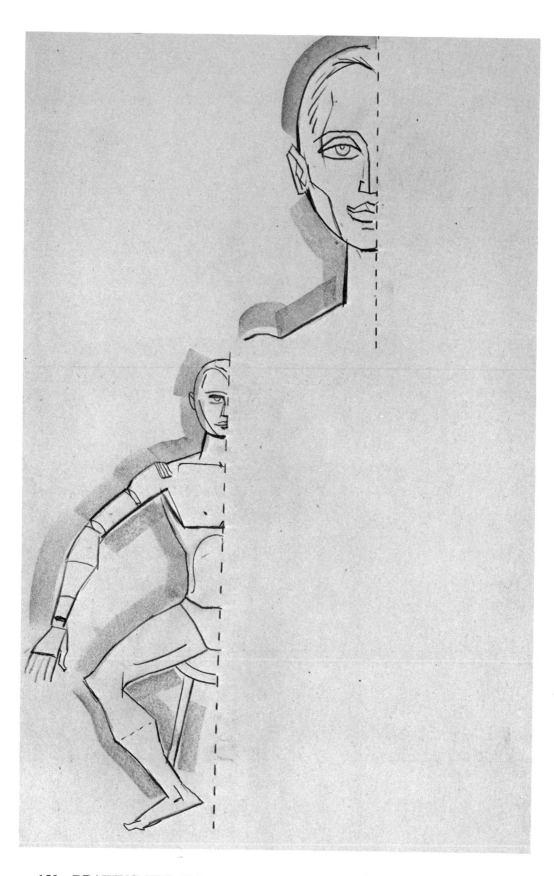

150 **DRAWING THE FIGURE FROM TOP TO TOE**

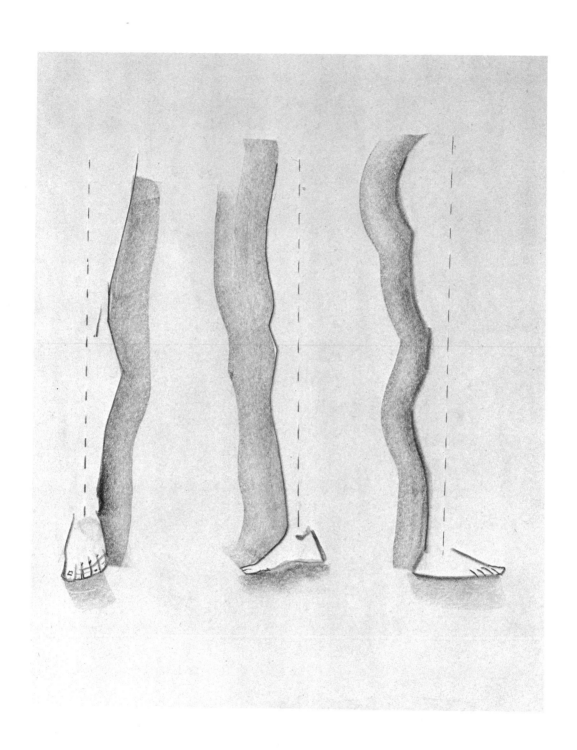

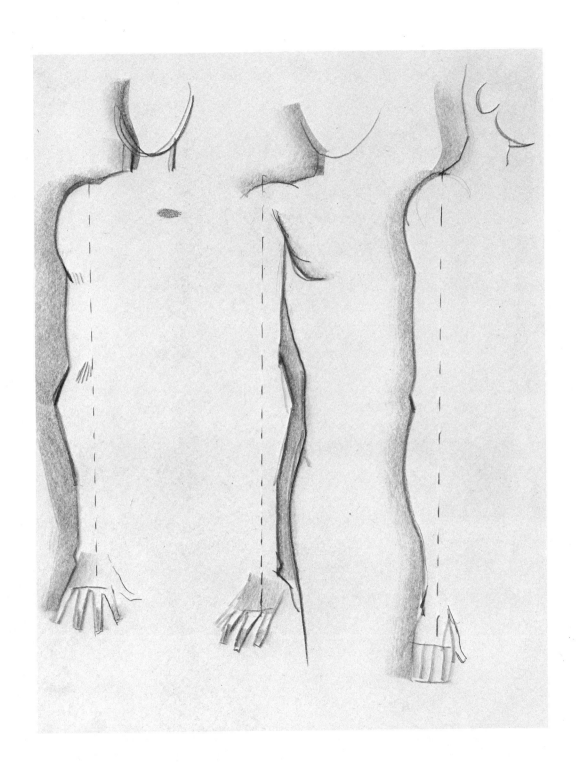